Just Gus

A Rescued Dog
And the Woman He Loved

By Laurie Williams

Photos by Roslyn Banish

Introduction by Jean Donaldson

McWittyPress • New York

Additional photos by:
Daniel Spirn: pages 16, 56, 57
Stephanie Williams: page 15
Marion Spirn: page 55
Nancy Marchetta: page 61

Designed by Kenneth B. Smith

Address inquiries to
McWitty Press, 110 Riverside Dr., 1A, New York, N.Y. 10024.
www.mcwittypress.com

ISBN 0-9755618-1-2

Printed in Hong Kong

10 9 8 7 6 5

For Stephanie, who showed us how precious life is.

The late paleontologist **Stephen Jay Gould** famously remarked that human brains can't comprehend large numbers. Unless we are mathematicians or astronomers, we tend to blank out once things get into the tens of thousands or above. So stating that "several million homeless dogs are killed in shelters every year in the United States" will fail to elicit the kind of reaction that an individual saga does. A simple story about one animal is something we can wrap our minds around. It is the inspiration for many of us who work in this field.

Several thousand dogs will be killed in animal shelters today—the day you're reading this. Every single one of those dogs had a story. They were born, they played, they looked forward to things, and they probably bonded to someone. For most of them, their luck ran out a few months—maybe a year—into their lives, when they got lethal injections at an animal shelter. Even worse, they may never have entered the shelter system and died harrowing deaths.

The story you're about to read is about one dog, Gus. He was born and then, somewhere along the line, he was lost or rejected. His luck started to run out in a big way when he suffered the universal "feel-bad" cliché: he was run over by a truck. What happened afterwards was as close to a miracle as dogs get on this planet. He dropped into the life of Stephanie Williams. Stephanie saved Gus. In return and with the effortless intensity that I think only dogs ever really achieve, Gus was there for Stephanie during a terminal illness.

The connection between human and dog has inspired scientific research, some of our oldest charities, and works such as the one you hold. Perfectly understood by all who've experienced it, it is hard to describe to those who've not. I admit to having a bit of an itch to make the latter group get it. I've even sometimes thought that there are people who should pretty much just be issued dogs: the elderly who are widowed, people seeking connection with life, retirees with feelings of diminished purpose, people who yearn for a greater link to the natural world. One look at Gus, steadfast with head on Stephanie's lap as she worked, is startlingly eloquent in regard to this bond. Dogs pay back in spades.

The good news for abandoned dogs is that their fate has been changing gradually. In some shelters, the "save rate"—the percentage of animals who enter the system and leave alive—has maxed out. This means that a healthy dog who is not dangerous has a 100% chance of being placed in a home if it has the good fortune to end up in one of these shelters. Furthermore, many dogs with mild to moderate health and behavior problems are rehabilitated and go on to be the apple of someone's eye.

There are shelters, such the one I work for, The San Francisco SPCA, that do even more. We go into classrooms to build empathy for animals in the next generation. Our hospital helps last-chance dogs like Gus. My own department is an academy where people train to become dog trainers and behavior counselors, because behavior is one reason people relinquish dogs. Our students come from all walks of life, but perhaps the most interesting are corporate cross-overs, those who might have chased status and money but then one day sat down and decided to pursue a career helping animals.

It is surely a sign of our ethical progress that the weakest and least valued members of our world—animals— are making headway. My wish is that all who read the story of Stephanie and Gus will be moved to rescue a dog, help out at a shelter, or make a donation.

Jean Donaldson
Founder and Director
The San Francisco SPCA Academy for Dog Trainers

Just Gus

Forgotten.

Alone.

Hungry and cold.

He was a young dog roaming the streets of the Bronx in the winter of 2003, dodging the dangers of a big city. Adrift and frightened, he survived as best he could. He was a dog with no name; a mutt, a scavenger, and a stray. And like thousands of other abandoned animals, he was headed toward a sad and anonymous end.

8

Any instincts or cunning that might have sustained this dog in a suburban or rural setting failed him in the tangle of New York streets. As bad as it was to be homeless, his fortune would take a turn for the worse before it got better.

Late one afternoon, he was hit by a truck, injured, and left for dead by the side of the road. He could have become just a statistic. This could have been the end of his story.

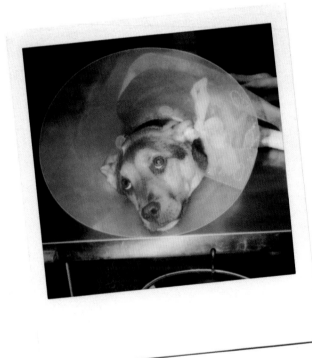

Luckily for the dog, a good Samaritan found him and, despite the late hour, brought him to a nearby animal hospital. What began as a good deed quickly became more complex. "I'm sorry, sir," explained the receptionist, "but we can't treat this dog unless you agree to pay for his care."

The man began to protest, making a scene in the waiting room. An intern, Jenna (a pseudonym), calmly explained that x-rays were needed to determine the extent of the injuries and that they would cost $160. The room fell silent. "I'll pay for the x-rays," murmured a man seated in the corner, a small sick bird in his hands. The other people relaxed and the rescuer, confident that the dog would be treated, headed home.

The x-rays revealed a serious leg fracture that would require the insertion of multiple pins and extensive physical therapy during recovery. Although sympathetic to the dog's situation, no one in the waiting room could afford the expensive surgery.

That's when Jenna took a gamble.

Jenna enlisted the services of the resident in charge of the surgical department, and together they performed the needed surgery "off the books." Carrying the poor dog between rooms, Jenna had been struck by his sweetness and composure, despite his obvious pain. His big brown eyes begged for help. She knew he was worth saving.

"He was a very lucky dog," she admitted. "Lucky that he survived the accident, lucky that a kind man found him and brought him in, lucky that someone paid for the x-rays, and lucky that I was working that night." After the operation, Jenna took the dog to her home in Brooklyn. She wanted to adopt him, but she already had a full house, with five strays taken in over the years. How would she find someone who could adopt an animal with so many needs on short notice?

Little did she know that the perfect person was right around the corner.

Stephanie Williams, an accomplished magazine writer and aspiring novelist, lived alone in the Park Slope neighborhood of Brooklyn. Two years earlier, at the age of 30, Stephanie had been diagnosed with advanced breast cancer. As the disease progressed, she was determined to accept the decline ahead with dignity.

But Stephanie didn't want to go it alone. "She knew that her family couldn't be there for her twenty-four hours a day," recalled her mother, Faye. "She wanted a constant companion. That's where she came up with the idea of adopting a shelter dog."

Because of her illness, most shelters were reluctant to let her adopt. Then she learned from friends about an injured mixed-breed in the neighborhood that was in desperate need of a home. Stephanie didn't hesitate. She called Jenna and told her how much she wanted a dog. Jenna was candid about the care the dog would need. "I was blown away by her story," related Jenna. "Steph was very matter-of-fact about her illness: 'You know, I might make it, I might not. But I have a supportive family behind me who will step in if they have to.'" That was good enough for Jenna, so they agreed to meet the next day.

Jenna and the dog approached Stephanie along a tree-lined street at the appointed hour. Stephanie's father, Larry, who was visiting at the time, observed: "As they walked toward us, I could see this poor dog, all skinny and limping. But he was friendly, and you couldn't help but look at his eyes. We felt so sorry for him."

While they walked together, Jenna offered to let Stephanie keep the dog overnight to see if they would be a good match. She also promised to provide any future veterinary services the dog might require. She really wanted to make the adoption possible. Jenna believed in the woman—just as she believed in the dog.

19

This pooch was a little larger than Stephanie's dream dog. He didn't easily fit on her lap, and toting him around in a handbag was out of the question. But the dog was a character; a craving for American cheese was just one of his charms. Fortunately, Stephanie had recently moved into an apartment with a small yard. It was just right for her convalescing pup, who spent his first afternoon sniffing every corner.

The first night, Stephanie slept beside him. "I knew he wouldn't be able to jump up in bed with me," Stephanie said. "So I arranged to sleep on the couch and put his bed on top of my coffee table, which I pulled right beside me."

Around three in the morning, the dog woke Stephanie with his whimpering. "I gently scratched his wound and he stopped whining immediately," she remembered. "Then he took one paw and placed it on my forearm. I looked into his eyes and at that moment I knew: This dog wasn't going back. He was meant to be my companion. Beat up as we both were, we were going to go through this life together."

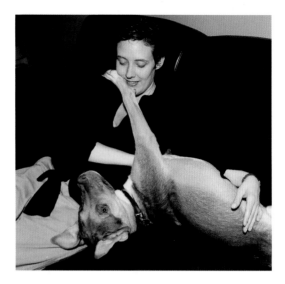

The dog made himself completely at home. "I wasn't planning to let him up on my furniture," Stephanie remembered. "But right away I realized, what was the use of having this dog if I couldn't lay him across my lap and pet him?"

First she ceded the leather couch. "He plopped down, stomach up," she recalled. "He might have been through a lot, but he was still trusting." Then he took over her blue chair, head draped over the armrest. "He looked so comfortable. I didn't have the heart to kick him out."

The furniture remained unharmed, but the same could not be said for a toothbrush, glasses, a watchstrap, and a cashmere sweater. As the dog's tastes expanded from cheese to prescription eyeware, tolerance became Stephanie's credo.

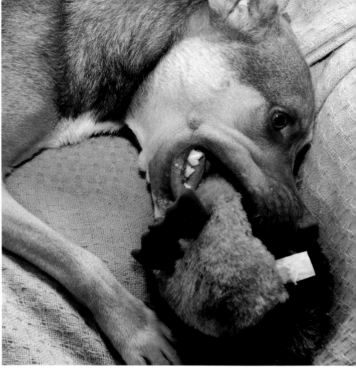

S tephanie stocked up on bones, chew toys, and a rope for tug-of-war. A dog with plenty of toys ignores cashmere, reasoned Stephanie.

In no time at all, the dog had developed a strategy for destroying stuffed animals. He'd chew the fur, bite at the seam, then pull out the stuffing. When he was finished, he let Stephanie know he was out of toys by eating gauze in the bathroom. New gauze was bought. New toys were bought. This was the system. "Stephanie told us not to spoil him," said her father, "but if you saw the cabinet full of treats and toys, you'd know who was spoiling the pup."

Since the dog was definitely staying, he needed a
fitting name. "Stephanie had actually settled on a
name months before even hearing about this dog,"
her mother recalled. "She loved the name Dew, which she
adopted from the Doolittle character in the film, *A Coal
Miner's Daughter*. She'd give it a good 'ol Southern drawl
for effect: Deeeew." But this moniker just didn't seem to fit the
soulful dog she had brought home.

Stephanie wanted a name that somehow honored
the dog's past hardships. So she turned to the country music
legends of her Texas youth. Hank? He drank too much, and
never from the toilet. Waylon? Too much of an outlaw, though
eating cashmere seemed criminal. Willie? The dog didn't
look good in braids. Then she remembered Augustus McRae
of Larry McMurtry's *Lonesome Dove*, the old cowboy who
wanted a second chance. It was a perfect fit. From that day
forward, Gus was Gus.

Gus gravitated toward people. "He stopped to say hello to everyone, especially small children," remembered Stephanie's father. "They wanted to meet him because he was so loveable." His quick handshake made Stephanie wonder if Gus was running for office.

"What kind of dog is he?" people would ask. Almost everyone volunteered an opinion. "He looks just like my brother's German Shepherd." Or, "You think he may have a little Rhodesian Ridgeback?" Stephanie consulted veterinarians and scoured websites looking for dogs resembling Gus. One week she was even convinced he was a Dogote: part dog, part coyote. There were lots of likely suspects, but never a positive identification. Eventually, Stephanie realized that Gus's heritage would remain a mystery. He was just Gus.

After each walk around the neighborhood, Stephanie would massage and stretch Gus's legs. As the days passed, she could see that he was limping less and getting stronger. He seemed eager to explore—and Stephanie knew the perfct place, a few blocks away from their home.

Just outside their small Brooklyn apartment, the vast 526 acres of Prospect Park beckoned. This rustic retreat in the center of New York's most populous borough offers large meadows, serene lakes, and dense forests.

For dog owners, it provides something more: officially sanctioned off-leash hours. Dogs are allowed to run free every morning until 9:00 a.m. For the dogs of New York, it doesn't get any better than this.

MANHATTAN

N

Stephanie's
apartment

BROOKLYN

PROSPECT PARK

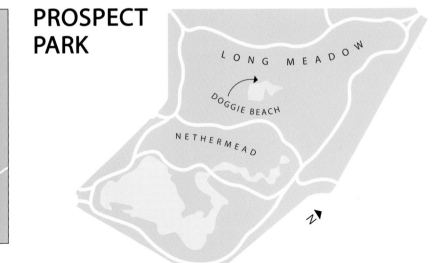

L O N G   M E A D O W

DOGGIE BEACH

N E T H E R M E A D

N

Under Stephanie's care, Gus healed quickly. As she watched him grow, Stephanie wondered about the progression of her own illness. She was losing weight, and her energy seemed to be fading. She felt scared sometimes, but she resolved to remain strong.

In just a few weeks, Gus was ready for his first trip to Prospect Park. Approaching the entrance, Stephanie didn't know what to expect. How would he respond to the wide-open spaces and the many new scents and sounds? She had delayed taking Gus to the park early in his recovery for fear of tempting him beyond his abilities. But the time seemed right. Gus was ready to make another leap back into living.

33

Stephanie let **Gus** take the lead as they entered the park. While they walked, they shared a growing sense of discovery: a whole new world in their own backyard. As if through Gus's eyes, Stephanie saw the sheer breadth of the park, the dogs running in the distance, and the dense greens and browns that surrounded them.

On the outskirts of the park, Gus inspected every rock, blade of grass, and stick in his path, occasionally leaving his scent to lay claim to his new turf. Eventually, their path led to a tunnel beneath an overpass. When the time was right, Stephanie unhooked Gus's leash and watched him charge through and gallop into Long Meadow on the other side. She had no desire to rein him in.

Throughout the meadow, there were dogs of every color, size, and breed. Gus watched the high-speed chases and tug-of-wars, eager to join in the fun. Soon he was sniffing with the best of them and rolling around like a big clown, happy to be the center of attention. Olive, a gray and white Old English Sheepdog, quickly became one of Gus's special friends. "Gus was like a big magnet," observed Nicole, Olive's human. "He was so gentle with Olive. They would see each other across the park and start running towards one another." Very *Casablanca*.

37

Gus and Stephanie became regulars at the park. Gus bonded with some of the larger dogs and formed what their humans dubbed "The Puppy Pack." The core members—Earl (clockwise), Nacho, Rosie, Flaco, and Gus—were almost inseparable. Many of the humans became close friends as well. They compared notes on movies and books, but most of the time they talked about their beloved pets. "Does Gussie need a winter coat?" Or, "What do you think of Science Diet?" One day Stephanie pulled out a red rubber ball, unintentionally luring Earl into an obsession. "He was still happy to see his friends," says Earl's human, "but fetching a red ball became his life's work."

The Puppy Pack liked to frolic at Doggie Beach, a stretch of sand, set aside specifically for dogs. along a small lake. Splashing about in the water just didn't come naturally to Gus, though. He would get his feet wet in the shallows, but wouldn't venture out deeper to swim, even when the other members of the pack were paddling around.

Stephanie finally decided to give him an extra nudge. Recalling the way she had "learned" how to swim, Stephanie turned to her father for help. He would pick Gus up, stand on two rocks at the edge of the beach, and toss Gus out into the water. Each time Gus would swim to shore, looking bedraggled but rather pleased with himself.

Big dogs come with big responsibilities, Stephanie realized. Gus might not be well bred, but he could certainly be well trained. She pored over books from the local library and picked up training tips from Gunni, the canine guru of Prospect Park. When Stephanie took Gus to obedience classes at a nearby school, he proved a quick learner. "He was the star of the class, a real teacher's pet," remembered a friend. "Stephanie led him around so proudly." Soon she had Gus and a posse of pooches hanging on her every word.

42

Dubbed the **"Mayor of Dogville,"** Gus had become one of the most popular dogs in the park. He relished the extra attention that came with his high office. Each morning he'd make the rounds, wagging his tail and nudging his two-legged friends for a little treat.

45

Satisfied, he'd let the games begin. "Gus could always be found where the action was," recalled Stephanie's father. "He would run around for an entire hour, but he always knew where Stephanie was. She would call, and he would come running."

Despite good training, Gus couldn't always curb his enthusiasm. After a rain, he'd run straight for the puddles of Prospect Park and all the mud he could find. He would stick his nose in it, roll in it, and even eat it. If he hadn't been called Gus, his name might have been Mud. Before owning Gus, Stephanie would have cringed at the sight of a muddy dog lunging her way. But like most dog lovers, she came to tolerate Gus's most outlandish activity—even if it left brown tracks across her hardwood floors.

Play in the mud; pay the price. Gus quickly learned that mud baths were always followed by real ones. Gus never put up a fight. Stephanie never complained. Stephanie's friends were amazed. "Whenever we talked, it was all Gus all the time," recalled her close friend Allis. "Gus rolled in the mud today, Gus has a girlfriend at the park, Gus is the pride of the neighborhood. She was convinced that Gus was the center of everyone's universe. With Gus, she was all sap, all the time."

Stephanie looked forward to her visits to the park just as much as Gus did. It was a much needed escape from the preoccuption with her health. "I sometimes found it tough to spend time with friends," wrote Stephanie, as the cancer began taking its toll. "It wasn't just the going out; it was the talking, the answering questions, the fact that I was always the center of attention when I just felt like curling up into a ball and disappearing."

Gus gave Stephanie and her friends a welcome new focus. His perpetual pep and goofy manner were a gift that allowed Stephanie and the others to forget about the hardships she faced. For Stephanie, forgetting was freedom.

At the park, Stephanie and Gus were part of a new community that neither questioned nor pitied. Stephanie was just another woman; Gus was just another dog. Their mornings were about living.

Although Stephanie didn't know Gus's precise birthday, she wanted to throw a party to mark their first anniversary together. Members of the Puppy Pack were invited, as well as family and friends and Stephanie's boyfriend, Daniel, who lived several hours away.

"Stephanie loved Gus so much that I really wanted to do something special for him," remembered her mom. "But how much can you do for a dog?" She decided to cook him his favorite food. "I bought a pound of liver and fried it up for him and his pals, with a few pieces of bacon and cheese on the side." The two-legged guests sang happy birthday and blew out the candles. The four-legged friends scarfed down their choice morsels.

Stephanie had met Daniel months before her cancer diagnosis. "I fell in love with his gentleness, his curiosity about the world," she once wrote. "Throughout a year filled with pain, radiation, and 12-hour surgeries, he made the four-hour drive from his home almost every weekend."

Daniel appreciated Gus's playfulness, his spirit, but most of all, the companionship he gave Stephanie. "I fell in love with the Gusser right away," Daniel remembered. "I never had a dog as a child, so he gave me an excuse to act like a kid again." On weekends they'd roughhouse, wrestle, and play tug-of-war, as Stephanie rooted for them both.

Writing a novel had always been Stephanie's greatest ambition. Cancer and a subsequent disability leave gave her the time—and the sense of urgency—to work hard at it. Writing became her goal and her solace, even as the cancer spread to her skin. "I woke up thinking about what my characters would do next rather than the red blotches that were making their way up my chest," she once wrote. Following their morning outings, Gus would cozy up next to Stephanie on the sofa as she worked on her laptop. When she felt weak, she would pull him close. He stayed by her side, comforting her through chemotherapy, fatigue, and even writer's block.

Writing continually through hospitalizations and days of treatment, Stephanie completed the first draft of *Enter Sandman* on New Year's Eve of 2003. "As awful as it is to have cancer, at least it has given me the time to work on my novel," wrote Stephanie later. "If I hadn't gotten sick, I would have put it off and probably never finished it. Cancer is allowing me to realize my dream."

During the early months of 2004, Stephanie's health rapidly declined. The cancer spread to her lungs, and she often needed oxygen in order to breathe. While she reserved most of her energy for morning walks with Gus, she was no longer able to take him to the park every day. To those around Gus, it seemed that he could sense the change and knew it was serious. "When Stephanie was on oxygen, she would sit on a bench in the park to rest and watch," recalled Nicole. "Gus would crawl up and sit beside her. Gus was like Steph's mom. He took care of her."

Stephanie's worsening condition was becoming obvious to her friends at Prospect Park. Still, Nicole did not realize how fast time was running out until one February day: "I heard her say, 'Gus, go play. This might be the last time I ever see snow, and I want to see you enjoy it.'"

Despite her weakening condition, Stephanie was determined to hold her novel in her hands before she died. She wanted to leave something meaningful behind. Most of all, she wanted to be remembered. So as the deadline approached, she worked her way through revisions from her hospital bed. Gus was never far from her thoughts. "She wanted to know every detail of his day," recalled her father. "Did you take Gus to the park today? Did he behave?" Just one account of Gus's activity wasn't enough for Stephanie. She frequently traded e-mails with her park buddies to monitor events in the meadow. She couldn't bear to miss one moment of Gus's life.

In June, Stephanie came home after an extended hospital stay. She was thrilled when the first copy of *Enter Sandman*—her novel about a life-changing misfortune and the power of friendship—arrived from the printer. It was a relief to know that her novel was on its way to bookstores. She said she was having the best time of her life, giving phone interviews and reading reviews. On June 14th, friends and family gathered at a book party to celebrate Stephanie's achievement. Although she had trouble breathing, Stephanie thanked the many people who had helped her along the way. There was silence after she told them: "I'm so happy that I feel like I've died and gone to heaven."

On July 3, 2004, Stephanie Williams died at Memorial Sloan-Kettering Hospital in Manhattan.

Weeks before her death, Stephanie completed an article entitled "Saying Goodbye to My Life." Published posthumously in *Glamour* magazine, the story gave voice to Stephanie's thoughts about her impending death. She wrote about her loved ones, her dreams, her fears, and the idea of remembrance. She wrote about Gus, too:

"Most of the time, I don't think about the things that really hurt. Like the day I'll say goodbye to my dog, Gus. He sleeps by my side, and puts his head on my shoulder; whenever I cry, he runs to lick my tears. He wakes me up every morning, first to cuddle and then, at eight o'clock sharp, to let me know it's time for our walk in the park. He keeps me company when the whole world goes on without me. How can I leave this dog? Already, during my long hospital stays, he gets confused. (Where is she? When's she coming back?) I wonder how many days, how many weeks, he will watch the door, waiting for me to come home."

63

Stephanie's death was heartbreaking for everyone who knew her. Gus was no exception. At first, he seemed anxious and confused. But gradually he seemed to be aware that Stephanie was not coming home. Daily outings to the park and visits from friends were welcome distractions for him, but the Brooklyn apartment was no longer a home without Stephanie.

Though a number of friends and family had offered to adopt Gus, Stephanie had chosen the person she believed would provide the best home for him: Daniel. With plans to move to Minneapolis for a new job, Daniel turned to several of Stephanie's friends to look after Gus during the summer until his new place was ready.

One of them was Jenna, the vet who had originally saved Gus. She told Stephanie's family: "I feel so blessed to have witnessed the growth of this relationship between Stephanie and Gus. It's the thing I feel best about in my career. If I never practice medicine again, I will be able to look back and say, 'that's why I did it.'"

Several months after Stephanie's death, Gus jumped into a car bound for Minneapolis. It was a journey halfway across the country that would represent a fresh start for both Daniel and Gus. Daniel had chosen their new home with Gus in mind. Says Daniel: "After searching all over the city, I finally found a house within walking distance of lakes, wooded areas, and one of the largest dog parks in the city. It was perfect."

When Gus first got to Minneapolis, he stuck very close. "At night he would curl up at the bottom of the bed," recalls Daniel. "It seemed to give him a feeling of security. It was comforting for me, too."

Daniel and Gus set about the task of moving on with their lives. Gus's new two-story house was much larger than his Brooklyn apartment had been, as was the sprawling, tree-lined yard. It took time, but the extra living space— indoors and out—aroused Gus's playful spirit. "After several weeks, he seemed to know that I wasn't going to leave him and that this was his permanent home," Daniel remembers. "Suddenly he was bounding around like a puppy again."

Gus was eager to explore the great outdoors. "I tried to do what I could to maintain some of Gus's basic routines," says Daniel. "We'd go to the large dog park near our house all the time, even in sub-freezing temperatures." But nothing made Gus happier than running free through the wooded trails. "It reminded me of his early days in Prospect Park," Daniel recalls fondly. "Gus is becoming the dog he was meant to be."

New beginnings can help overcome old fears. "I was so proud the day Gus learned to swim," says Daniel. "We went out into Cedar Lake together. I gently lifted his stomach up out of the water until he got comfortable, then backed away and made him paddle to me." From then on, swimming in lakes and the Mississippi River became one of Gus's favorite activities. Dog tossing was no longer required.

emory are wonderful and mysterious. Sometimes they fade, only to be stirred up in the most unexpected ways. Watching Gus, Daniel often wonders what memories are triggered by his senses. Does he think of Olive when he sniffs a new dog? Does a big field remind him of Prospect Park? When he dozes off, does he ever dream he's on Stephanie's sofa? "I think of Stephanie often," says Daniel, "and I think Gus does too."

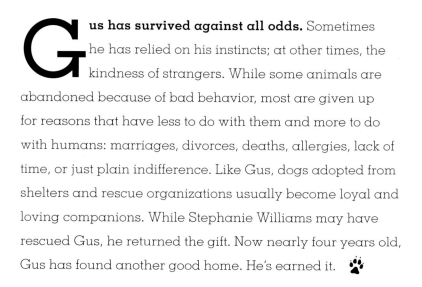

Gus has survived against all odds. Sometimes he has relied on his instincts; at other times, the kindness of strangers. While some animals are abandoned because of bad behavior, most are given up for reasons that have less to do with them and more to do with humans: marriages, divorces, deaths, allergies, lack of time, or just plain indifference. Like Gus, dogs adopted from shelters and rescue organizations usually become loyal and loving companions. While Stephanie Williams may have rescued Gus, he returned the gift. Now nearly four years old, Gus has found another good home. He's earned it.

If you are interested in adopting a dog, contact your local animal shelter or rescue organization.

To learn about the many shelters and organizations caring for homeless animals, contact one of the following groups:

San Francisco Society for the Prevention of Cruelty to Animals
Finds loving homes for homeless cats and dogs; programs include a full-service veterinary hospital, Spay/Neuter clinic, Academy for Dog Trainers, dog training classes, and a comprehensive Humane Education program.
www.sfspca.org

North Shore Animal League of America
The largest no-kill shelter in the U.S., located in New York state, this group rescues animals and has an on-line photo gallery of those awaiting adoption.
www.nsalamerica.org

Hugs for Homeless Animals
A directory of animals available for adoption from many different shelters nationwide and worldwide.
www.h4ha.org

Hearts United for Animals
An animal welfare organization that rescues dogs from all over the country and specializes in long-distance adoptions.
www.hua.org

Petfinder
An on-line database that provides names of shelters and adoptable animals by type, region, and zip code, along with photos and profiles.
www.petfinder.org

Pets 911
Sponsored by the Animal Planet network, this database lists lost pets and provides extensive information on animals available for adoption across the country.
www.pets911.com

Rescue Workers Adoption
A webpage for canine and feline rescue workers nationwide to showcase some of the animals available for adoption.
www.adoptablepets.net

1-800-Save-A-Pet
A non-profit pet adoption charity that helps shelters, humane societies, SPCA's, and pet rescue groups advertise homeless pets to potential adopters.
www.1-800-save-a-pet.com

Pet Harbor
Specializes in lost and found pets, as well as animals that need to be adopted.
www.Petharbor.com

Best Friends Animal Society
A Utah-based organization that cares for 1,500 animals and promotes its "No More Homeless Pets" campaign.
www.bestfriends.org